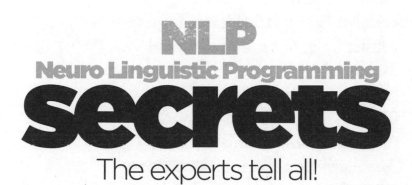

NLP
Neuro Linguistic Programming
secrets
The experts tell all!

About the author
Carolyn Boyes MA (Hons), DCH,
Master Practitioner and Certified
Trainer of NLP

Carolyn is a coach and the author
of *Communication* and *Career
Management*, also in the **business
secrets** series, and other books
published by HarperCollins,
including *Cool Careers, Need to
Know? NLP* and *Need to Know?
Cognitive Behavioural Therapy.*

NLP
Neuro Linguistic Programming
secrets

Collins
A division of HarperCollins*Publishers*
77-85 Fulham Palace Road, London W6 8JB

www.BusinessSecrets.net

First published in Great Britain in 2010 by HarperCollins*Publishers*
Published in Canada by HarperCollins*Canada*. www.harpercollins.ca
Published in Australia by HarperCollins*Australia*. www.harpercollins.com.au
Published in India by HarperCollins*PublishersIndia*. www.harpercollins.co.in

4

Copyright © HarperCollins*Publishers* 2010

SECRETS and BUSINESS SECRETS are trademarks of HarperCollins*Publishers*

Carolyn Boyes asserts the moral right to be identified as the author of this work.

A catalogue record for this book is available from the British Library.

ISBN 978-0-00-734675-2

Printed and bound at Clays Ltd, St Ives plc

CONDITIONS OF SALE

Mixed Sources
Product group from well-managed
forests and other controlled sources
www.fsc.org Cert no. SW-COC-001806
© 1996 Forest Stewardship Council
FSC

FSC is a non-profit international organisation established to promote the
responsible management of the world's forests. Products carrying the FSC
label are independently certified to assure consumers that they come
from forests that are managed to meet the social, economic and
ecological needs of present and future generations.

Find out more about HarperCollins and the environment at
www.harpercollins.co.uk/green

Contents

NLP secrets

Learn how to use NLP in business

Neuro Linguistic Programming (NLP) is a method used in business to improve performance. It contains techniques that help to change your patterns of thoughts, emotions and behaviour in positive ways. You can use these techniques for yourself, or as a manager with your team.

I first learnt these techniques 15 years ago while I was working in international sales. Immediately I realized how dramatically my performance would improve by applying them in my business work and other parts of my life. I trained first as a practitioner and then as a teacher of NLP. I have since coached and trained hundreds of business people in NLP methods and ways of thinking.

NLP began life in the 1970s as the result of studies at the University of California. Richard Bandler and John Grinder came up with a model of human excellence based on their research into language and behaviour, and the link between mind and body.

NLP has become a powerful tool for improving performance. Some of the benefits I have observed in myself and others are better communication and team skills, overcoming blocks to performance, improved sales, management and leadership skills, greater self-confidence, improved presentation and influencing skills, and the ability to generate clearer goals and achieve them.

This book consists of 50 **secrets** about NLP, divided into seven chapters.

■ **Take responsibility.** The basic thinking in NLP that allows you to focus on the results you want to get in business.
■ **Focus on your outcome.** How to set a clear desired outcome in order to improve short- and long-term performance.
■ **Be an excellent communicator.** Tools that help you to have better relationships with your colleagues and clients.
■ **Be a great motivator.** Understand how to motivate yourself and others, and achieve more.
■ **Boost your performance.** Overcome barriers and blocks to performance, and increase your personal power in business.
■ **Make a powerful impression.** Increase the impact you make in meetings and at presentations.
■ **Sell to anyone.** How to sell yourself, your products and your ideas successfully inside and outside your organization.

If you follow these 50 **secrets**, you will have learnt the ways of thinking that allow business leaders to become star business performers. Look forward to boosting your business performance every day and avoid the pitfalls that can hold you back from success.

You can change your results just by changing the way you think.

Take responsibility

The key attitude that underlies the thinking and techniques of NLP is to take charge of what happens to you. Once you decide to take responsibility for your business success you will achieve more of what you want (and less of what you don't want). When you don't get the result you want quickly, you'll find it easier to uncover the block and know what to do about it.

1.1

Be 'at cause'

"I can't help being late. All my family are like that."
"I can't do anything about getting on with my boss.
It's him who always causes the problems." "I can't
make this business successful, the economy is too
bad." "I can't stop smoking, I'm addicted to
smoking." "It's not my fault!"

Everything that happens in life has a cause. Ben eats a big meal.
What happens? He puts on weight. Krizia doesn't eat for two days, and
loses weight? It's simple: the effect of eating too much or too little has
been caused by the action of eating too much or too little.

■ **The Cause: Effect equation.** NLP expresses this with the Cause:
Effect equation, C:E. Cause is on one side, and Effect is on the other.

one minute wonder Any time you feel unsure about
what you are doing, take a minute to think about
what you want to achieve. By being clear about the
outcome you want, you will soon understand what
you need to take responsibility for. This will make you
more prepared to be 'at cause' in business.

"Always bear in mind that your own resolution to succeed is more important than any other"

Abraham Lincoln, 19th-century US President

What this means is that for every cause there is an effect and for every effect there is a cause.

■ Are you at the cause of your life or the effect of your life? In other words, do you take responsibility for what happens to you or do you consider yourself a passive victim?

Losing weight's a simple example. Take responsibility, exercise more and eat less, and see if you get a different result. Probably you will. Occasionally it gets more complicated, if there's a medical issue for example, but then you can stay 'at cause' by taking medical advice. Now you know how to lose weight again.

But what about my relationship with my boss? Why is it not working? The original cause may not be as obvious. Was it me or him? Or both of us? All you know is that it's not working. So how do you stay on the cause side of the equation on this one?

Well, at first glance it may not seem an easy situation to change, but in fact it's very simple. All you have to do to be 'at cause' is to take responsibility for the results you get from now on. So what if it was his fault? How about changing your beliefs about the situation and behaving differently towards him? See what happens. Later secrets will give you great tools for doing this.

Decide to be in charge of your business success, and not at the mercy of what happens to you.

1.2

Know your map

In ancient times, sailors set out to explore the world. The maps they drew up look very different to maps made today in the era of satellite navigation. The ancient mariners' perception of the world was clearly different from ours. Future generations will also have different maps and ideas about the cosmos as technology evolves. This illustrates a central idea of NLP: that a map – and thus our peception of the world – is always subjective.

In other words, each of us has a unique view on the world. How we see the world is not actually how the world is, it's simply the internal map (or model) we've developed – our way of looking at things. Each of us may think we are looking at things as they really are, but the way we think is just a viewpoint. Someone else may think very differently about the same situation.

■ **The role of the subconscious.** Most of the time, how we think about things is subconscious. It has to be, because the conscious mind can focus only on a few things at a time. Subconsciously we take in much more. Our subconscious runs our body, stores our memories and

one minute wonder Always have respect for another person's view of the world. Just because someone disagrees with you or has different values, that doesn't mean that they are wrong (or you are wrong) – simply that you have different maps.

takes in information through the senses. We're bombarded with information – some say two million bits of it per second, whereas consciously we're only aware of about seven bits of information per second. That's why our internal map of the world is unique. Without thinking about it, we pay attention to some things more than others.

Once you recognize that your map is a subjective view of the world, you can begin to do two useful things.

 Firstly, recognize that other people's views are equally subjective and valid.

Secondly, look inside yourself and work out what you are choosing to pay attention to.

Once you start to perceive the things around you that you've previously been ignoring, then you have the choice to change your map if your current one isn't getting you to the destination you want.

If you change the way you think, you'll change the way you act. If you change the way you act, you'll change the results you get.

We each have a unique internal map of the external world.

1.3

Look below the surface

All the time you are reading this there is a lot going on below the surface. In the few seconds it has taken you to read this far into Secret 1.3, your subconscious has already been very busy. You weren't aware of what was going on. So what's happening?

Your brain acts as a virtual reality machine. As you are reading this Secret you are taking in information through your senses: seeing, hearing, feeling, smelling and tasting. You are probably most aware of your visual sense, but the others are still working hard as well.

The subconscious interprets the information it receives and stores some of it as memories.

one minute wonder Bear in mind that the body and mind are linked. What you think affects what you feel. What you feel affects what happens inside your body and, in turn, your body language and your behaviours which are visible to other people. So how you think ultimately influences how other people react to you.

Three big filters are always being used by the subconscious:

1 Deletion. First of all your subconscious promptly deletes most of the information it receives. That's why you don't remember the two million bits of information you are smelling, hearing and feeling as you are reading this. For example, how aware are you of the feeling in your arms or legs? Maybe you are now, but were you a few seconds ago?

2 Distortion. At the same time you continually distort some of the information to store it more easily. For example, while travelling through the countryside you see a pretty cottage, which reminds you of a picture you once saw of a fairytale house made of gingerbread. Later, you don't remember the exact colour and details of the house, only a sense of it as the fairytale house.

3 Generalization. The subconscious groups information into categories. For example you see someone sitting on something that looks roughly like another object you habitually call a chair. "Hey", says your subconscious! "That's useful. I will describe this as a chair as well." (Even if the object is actually something else.)

Your subconscious always works hard for you, but its habit of distorting, deleting and generalizing all give rise to beliefs and opinions about the world that may not always be useful to you.

What can you do about it? First of all, start paying attention to your beliefs, and actively adopt and emphasize those beliefs that empower rather than limit your business success.

Your subconcious filters bits of information to create your highly personal view of the world.

1.4

Recognize your preferred sense

Each day we experience the world through the five senses. These are known as the *Visual*, or seeing, sense; the *Auditory*, or hearing, sense; the *Kinesthetic*, or touch and feeling, sense; the *Olfactory*, or smell, sense; and the *Gustatory*, or taste, sense. People rely on these five senses to different degrees.

We store representations of the outside world inside our subconscious using our senses. This is how a memory can bring back a smell, picture or sound. In NLP the senses are called representational systems.

We each subconsciously use one sense more than the others. Some store memories primarily as images. Others delete more of what they see, and store more sound images. If you subconsciously prefer the visual sense you may be drawn towards visual work. If you're more sound focused, then you may be especially fascinated by music or language. Or perhaps you prefer touch and feeling, and so favour physical pursuits, such as sport or working with your hands.

Just because you have a preference for one sense over another doesn't mean that you can't use all of them. This affects learning differences. If you prefer the visual, you may want visual props when

one minute wonder Be careful how you present information to others in business. Listen to the language the other person is using and use similar language back to them. If you are not sure about someone's preferred systems, make sure you present in a range of ways to cover different groups. Don't use only your preferred style.

learning. Auditory learners need to hear information to take it in efficiently. Kinesthetic learners like to try out what they are learning, for example through exercises and role play.

People give away their preferred sense through the words they choose. Use their preferred words and they will relate to you better. For example:

■ **Visual words.** Look, see, clear, bright, sparkling, picture, clarify, perspective, illustrate, focus, colourful, watch, illusion, shine, dim, vivid.
■ **Auditory words.** Noise, hear, rcsonate, deaf, speak, rhythm, ask, silent, tune, pitch, buzz, audible, earful, remark, tongue-tied, rings a bell.
■ **Kinesthetic words.** Feel, unfeeling, solid, concrete, hit, pressure, hothead, handle, soft, hard, cold, tickle, seize, pressure, get in touch with.

By finding out which senses you and your colleagues individually prefer, you can learn about your different maps of the world, different learning styles and how to communicate more flexibly.

People vary in the way they perceive the world through the different senses.

1.5

Discover your beliefs

Many of us use phrases like "It's true that…", "That is wrong", "That is totally right…", "I believe that…", "Well that's a matter of opinion, but this is indisputable…", "My opinion is…", "According to my perspective…". These are all statements of beliefs.

According to your model of the world something may appear to be a fact when it is really a very deeply held belief.

As we grow up we begin to take on views of the world. We can't help doing this. We have to believe something otherwise there would be just too much raw information swishing about. As we develop beliefs we often tend to focus on the information that supports our existing beliefs so they become stronger. It tends to be less often that we notice information that undermines existing beliefs and disproves them.

one minute wonder 'Am/am not' statements are a great way to uncover subconscious beliefs. Listen out for people making statements like: I am… I am not…; My friends are… my friends are not…; Life is… life is not…; The world is… the world is not…; Business is… business is not…; My future is… my future is not… .

> # "It doesn't matter where you are coming from. All that matters is where you are going."
>
> **Brian Tracy, performance coach**

If you hold lots of deep beliefs it can make you very rigid in your thinking and give rise to other strong opinions. It may result in an inflexible model of the world. If you have very rigid beliefs you may clash with other people who hold very different models of the world. Just think about some of the great conflicts in the wider world. They take place between different groups who firmly believe their opinions to be right and who cannot find a meeting place with their enemies' beliefs.

You can begin to uncover your beliefs very simply. Just ask yourself:

■ What do I believe about business / work / other areas?
■ Or write down, "I believe … (about this area of my life). I do not believe … (about another area)."

This will uncover some basic beliefs that you might not have been fully conscious of.

If you want to change the results in your life, then scrutinize your beliefs. If they are blocking your success, then start thinking about what other beliefs might be useful to you.

Identify your beliefs and ask yourself if they support you in being successful.

1.6

Identify your business values

What's important to you in business? What would make you stay in a job? What draws you to particular groups of people or a particular political cause? Is there anything that would make you uncomfortable ethically in business? What do you have in common with the people you get on with at work?

Our values are such an important part of our internal world that they pull us towards or away from situations and people throughout our lives. They are first formed in childhood, and influenced by family and friends. We may change our values according to experience as we grow older. But some values are so deeply held that we may be reluctant to change them and would rather leave a situation and uphold our values rather than compromise them.

■ **A value is anything that is important to you.** Stop and ask yourself: What's important to me about my job? The people I work with? My goals? Working for a great boss? Business? Values might include, for example, happiness, friendship, joy, learning, challenge, success. Whatever words you come up with are the right ones for you.

Often the deep values don't come to mind immediately, but they're the ones that really matter when important decisions have to be made. If you have ever felt forced to leave a job or come out of a relationship, think about what made you do it. Which value was lacking or wrong in the situation you came out of? Or which value did you want more of? These are the most important values to you.

By identifying your values in different parts of your life you will learn a lot about your subconscious motivations. You will discover what guides you to success and what may block you from time to time. When you have an outcome you think you want to achieve, but you keep sabotaging your success, it's always worth examining your values. It could be that you have two values that are clashing – motivating you in two contradictory directions. By identifying this, you have the opportunity to do something about it.

Identify what's important to you at work so you know where to put your focus and effort for the future.

1.7

Be observant

NLP has a term called sensory acuity. This is the ability to be highly observant. The more you notice in your world, the more you can fine-tune your actions and responses to fit situations in the most appropriate ways. This will in turn help you to achieve your goals.

The secret is to be observant of everything:

1 Notice what is happening with other people. Learn to notice changes in their behaviour, their communication and gradually to their subconscious body language.

one minute wonder Assuming that something has to be done or should be done limits choice and flexibility. A good way to counteract this is to acknowledge that there are always choices in any given situation. This puts you at the cause rather than the effect of any situation. Looking for choices and possibilities means that you will focus on the future and take responsibility for your success.

"All our dreams can come true, if we have the courage to pursue them" Walt Disney, American film producer

2 Become aware of your own behaviour and communication. Notice how you respond to events and circumstances. Become aware of what triggers different responses in you.

3 Become highly aware of what is going on inside your head. What are you thinking and feeling? What happens in the world when you change what you think and feel?

You will probably begin to notice changes in the way people look and how they sound. You may also begin to notice differences in the way you feel and the sounds and pictures you have in your head. In the next set of secrets you will learn how to explore your internal communication in more detail.

As you become more tuned into your ability to be observant, you may notice that this gives you greater ability to be flexible in your behaviour. The proof of your success will be in the quality of each outcome you achieve. Practise using your sensory acuity each day and see what results you achieve.

Fine-tune your sensory acuity and observe what you think and feel in different circumstances.

Focus on your outcomes

Some people have a vague idea of what they want. Some just drift. However, to get results in business, whether day-to-day or over a 10-year period or more, you need to have a clear vision of what you want to achieve. In NLP, the term 'outcome' is often used for what you define as the positive consequences of your actions. 'Outcomes' are more than just about setting yourself some goals, they are about understanding what it takes to achieve them.

Have well-formed visions

What results do you want? Do you have a clear picture in your head of what you want to achieve? Or are you someone who has a confused picture that keeps changing, or a picture of what you *don't* want, or barely any picture at all, just vague ideas? Which vision will achieve most?

People often wonder why they aren't successful. The real question is, are they successful in getting the result they really want or a result they hadn't planned and don't like?

The outcome you want can only happen when you have a well-formed vision of it. Once you've got a clear picture you'll be able to take the necessary steps to achieve it.

This is how to do it. Think of something you want to have, to be or to do in your life. Now ask these questions:

1 **Is it positive?** Focus on what you want, not what you don't want. (Otherwise, your internal picture will be of what you want to avoid and ironically that's probably what you'll end up with).

"If what you are doing is not moving you towards your goals, then it's moving you away from your goals" **Brian Tracy, performance coach**

 Is it specific? The more specific it is, the easier it'll be to focus on and you'll find it easier to know when you are near or far away from your goal.

 What is my evidence? How will I know when I have it? What will it look like? What will it feel like? If you don't have evidence you won't know when you have achieved your result.

 Who is in charge of this outcome? The answer has to be you, because an outcome dependent on others isn't achievable by you.

 Is this good for you? Will getting this result be good for you and your world as a whole? Consider the effect on you, others around you and your life.

 What resources do you have and need? Consider where you are in relation to your desired outcome. What do you have available to achieve this and what do you need to acquire?

Make sure that you build clear pictures in your mind of what you want to achieve.

2.2

Don't just try... DO it

"That's a great idea. I'll really try to take it on board." "I will try to meet you at 3pm. I know I didn't make the meeting last time but I will really make sure I try to get there in time for it today." "I am trying you know. I am really, really trying."

■ **'Trying' means two things.** In English the word 'trying' has two meanings: to attempt to do something, or to be a little upsetting, difficult or annoying.

Well, people who are always trying to do things can end up being extremely annoying to everyone else (and often themselves as well by the way). This is because they tend to let people down.

one minute wonder If you have any doubts about whether you really want the goals you are seeking, ask these questions: What will happen when you have it? What will happen if you don't have it? What won't happen when you have it? What won't happen if you don't have it? What are the benefits of not having it? What are the drawbacks of having it?

"Action is the foundational key to all success" Pablo Picasso, pioneering modern artist

■ **'Try' often implies failure.** There is a big difference between saying "I will get to the meeting by 3pm" and "I will try to get to the meeting by 3pm". Somehow we all know that the first person will only fail to get to the meeting under exceptional circumstances, but the second person will probably turn up late or perhaps not even make it at all.

There's also a big difference between saying "I will try to achieve what I have set out in my well-formed outcome in this area of my life" and "I will just do it. I will do what it takes to achieve this result. Maybe I am not clear exactly how I will do it yet but I will learn as I go along."

■ **Back to cause and effect.** Are you going to try to take responsibility for the results you get? Or are you going to take responsibility for the results you get? Are you going to try to lose weight… again? Or are you going to lose weight? Are you going to try to get a good relationship with your boss and grumble when you don't, or are you going to achieve that good relationship?

When you stop trying, that's when you really do start using whatever happens to you as feedback and take infinitely flexible actions to achieve your well-formed vision of success.

'Trying' implies failure, so leave out this word when defining your business goals.

2.3

Commit and take action

Lots of people want things. They want to have more success. They want to have more possessions. They want to have less stress. They want to have happier days, a bigger business, less debt, more money, more skills... The list goes on and on.

But a want is just a want. A want is meaningless in terms of achievement if you don't first turn it into a specific goal – or projected outcome – and then take action to get it.

■ What are you going to begin with right now to get what you want?

Your well-formed goals all need to start with a first step that turns into a second step and a third and a fourth and so on until you achieve what you set out to achieve.

This doesn't mean that you have to know everything you are going to *do* to get the result you want. It's more important that you know *what* you want first – your desired outcome – and then decide that you're going to do whatever it takes to get it.

"Unless commitment is made, there are only promises and hopes... but no plans"

Peter Drucker, business strategist

So there are two parts to this secret to success to remember.

- Firstly, to take action.
- Secondly, to commit 100% to the action.

It's no point doing something half-heartedly; you'll be back to 'trying', and you know how 'trying' that will be for you and other people.

Focus on your well-formed vision of outcome, take responsibility for the effect you wish to cause and take an action towards it. If you get a block on the way, take this as feedback and carry on taking action. Commit to your wanted outcome until you achieve the success you intended. This is what all people who achieve excellence do.

This doesn't mean that you can't adapt your vision of the outcome, of course. If your feedback gives you cause to think that you would prefer to achieve a different outcome, then change your goal. Take your new vision of outcome through the same set of questions as before and take a new first step. However, the principle remains the same. Whatever your projected outcome is, commit to it and the actions you take to achieve it. Do that and you will get the success and excellent results you want to achieve.

Take action to start achieving your goals from the moment you define them and keep moving forwards.

2.4

Break old habits

How much are you a creature of habit? Do you ever do different things, learn new skills, take on new work responsibilities? How often do you think differently? How curious are you? How experimental are you? If you do what you have always done you will get the same results you have always got.

Having an attitude of curiosity and experimentation can lead you to new, successful and exciting results in your life.

■ **People who are curious tend to ask lots of questions.** Perhaps they want to know what works, what could be different, how to create change, how other people do things. The more curious you become the better. Cultivate an attitude of curiosity. Consider how you do

one minute wonder Ditch your assumptions. We often pre-judge situations or people in advance. We don't bother to start things because we think we know exactly what result we are going to get in advance. Change your attitude, on the other hand, and you could change your life.

"It is in your moments of decision that your destiny is shaped"

Tony Robbins, self-help writer

things, for example, and how you could do things more effectively in future. What can you learn from other people?

■ The founders of NLP had this attitude. Richard Bandler and John Grinder wanted to know why certain people were more effective than other people, so they asked questions to find out. Their answers provided the thinking and techniques of NLP. What would happen if you asked questions about the world around you? Or what could you discover about your internal world?

■ Learn something new today. You might discover inner strengths and abilities that you were previously unaware of. Apply different ways of doing things and see what happens. It is only when you see the results from different actions that you can see the benefit of one route versus another. So break some habits. Experiment with the techniques and ways of thinking in this book.

■ Identify a business role model. Think about how they would make your job work better. Now do what they would do.

What will happen? You don't know yet, but you may be curious to find out. The one thing you absolutely know will happen is that breaking old habits will increase your choice and opportunities in life.

Experimenting will help you achieve greater long-term business success.

2.5

Use failure as feedback

What do you do when things don't work out as you want? Do you give up and moan about how terrible life is or do you pick yourself up and carry on? Do you keep working to achieve your goals or do you decide they must be unachievable because of the hurdles you face?

Another key idea underlying NLP is that:

■ There is no failure, only feedback.

When you are at the cause side of the cause: effect equation then anything that happens to you is good news. Even if it's a setback, you can learn from it and gain skills. So you didn't get the result you wanted. That doesn't mean you will never get the result you want. It may be that the way you set about getting it wasn't the best way. Maybe it's time

"Failure is success if we learn from it" Malcolm Forbes, publisher of 'Forbes' magazine

one minute wonder Be flexible. Practise going outside your comfort zone so that you gain a broader range of responses to what happens to you. Having set habits is limiting. If you do what you've always done, you will achieve what you've always achieved and find your successes limited to the successes you have had in the past.

to try something new. Or consider that you'll eventually get the result you want but your original time frame wasn't long enough.

Let's take a fitness example. You were unfit and wanted to be able to run around the park within two weeks. You didn't reach the goal. You almost did, but at the last minute your leg seized up.

■ Have you failed? No, you've just had some useful feedback.

If you rest or do some physiotherapy and lots of stretches next time, then you'll eventually get round that park.

Now back to that difficult boss. You've smiled at him every morning with no response. You still feel you have a bad relationship. You must have failed because what you did didn't get the result you wanted.

But you don't have to think so negatively. Instead, think: what could I do differently next time? Do I have a clear vision of how I want my relationship with him to be? Ah, that's right, I can suggest taking on that extra project. Let's see what happens.

As long as you are flexible in the actions you take, eventually you will get a different result.

Learn from your failures to identify what you need to grow your abilities.

2.6

Ask questions

Have you noticed how many questions there are in this chapter? Did you wonder why or did it just pass you by? If you ask the right questions they can lead to all sorts of useful thoughts. On the other hand, the wrong questions can have the opposite effect.

Think about what happens if you ask questions like, "Why do I always do badly at tasks my manager gives me?" The result is probably that you will find lots of reasons to *justify* why you do badly, and the situation won't change. This is sometimes referred to as the 'blame frame'. On the other hand, think about what might happen if you change the emphasis of the question to "How can I do better next time when I do a similar task?" Or "How can I learn from this so I can improve next time?" This is known as the 'outcome frame' in NLP.

case study After Kenny learnt NLP he started focusing on goals rather than his problems. Kenny used to ask himself, "Why am I no good at marketing in my job?" The answers he came up with were: "I don't like some of the people I have to market to. They're offhand with me, so I'm not going to try hard with them. And I'm shy; I avoid talking with strangers."

■ **'How?' is a great start to a question.** By asking how something is done, you can find out a lot about what works and what doesn't work. "How did he get that client to buy from him?" "How does he always get better results at the end of the month than his colleagues?" "How do I get better at what I do?" 'How' questions help you find the steps needed to achieve a particular result or type of behaviour. For example, have you ever wondered how someone who is at the top of your industry managed to achieve so much more than others who started work at the same time? Wouldn't that be a useful question to ask yourself?

■ **'What?' is a great follow-up question.** "What specifically makes the difference between succeeding and not succeeding in my business?" "What could I do that would make the biggest difference to my success?" "What do I want as an outcome?" "What do I need to change?"

Have you noticed just how useful and powerful these questions can be? Remember: the quality of your questions determines the quality of the answers.

If you're not getting the results you want, ask 'how and what' questions to find out what you can do differently.

However, after he set a well-formed vision of good communication, he started asking 'how?' questions instead. "How can I speak assertively and communicate more effectively with my boss?" "What I lost," Kenny says, "are all the justifications I used to have for not doing as well as I wanted. Instead I learnt how to market better. Six months later I was promoted!"

2.7

Be specific

Think about when you need to buy a plane, train or bus ticket. Would you ever consider not being specific about where you wanted to go? Well, there might be the odd occasion when you think, "I don't care where I end up", but most of the time we really do care. Business results are like tickets.

The word 'specific' is one of the most useful words you can use if you want to have more success in business.

■ **Reasons to be specific.** First of all, think about your personal or business goals and the results you want to achieve. What do you think happens if you are not at all specific about your desired outcome?

one minute wonder As you read through this book, bear in mind how you are going to take on board these NLP business secrets. Which specific secrets in this book will be most useful to you? How specifically will you apply them? Where specifically and when specifically will you use them?

Rather like buying a ticket without being clear about the destination, you'll end up somewhere and you'll definitely achieve something, but it's just down to luck if you get a result you like or one you don't.

Suppose you're a banker and a customer comes to you with a business plan, saying, "We plan to make between $100 and $1,000,000 within maybe two to five years, though we can't be sure how much and when…" Would you lend this customer money? No.

Or suppose you buy a plane ticket to "anywhere in Africa" while secretly hoping you might end up in Zambia. It would of course be best to buy a ticket to Zambia in the first place. In the same way, make sure you have a specific outcome to focus on now. The more specifically you plan, the more precisely you'll achieve.

Being specific is also useful when you want to change something which doesn't work. Here are some questions you can practise:

■ What specifically have you learnt in your business life that has led you to where you are? What specifically do you think you need to learn to progress even further?
■ What specific habits are useful and what specifically would you like to change?

See what happens when you get more specific with your business outcomes and your personal and professional development goals.

Be specific about what you want. A vague starting point can only give you a vague result.

Be an excellent communicator

Good communication is fundamental to NLP. In business, whether you are dealing with clients or with colleagues, your ability to get your message across is vital. You communicate all the time, through your body language, words and voice. Whether you're face-to-face or at a distance, your communication influences other people's reaction to you. Practise the NLP techniques in this chapter to be an excellent communicator.

Establish rapport

"That meeting went well. We were all on the same wavelength." "I felt really in tune with her." "That negotiation was really easy, we all seemed to be on the same page."

Rapport is that wonderful feeling you get of chemistry, relaxation and a sense of comfort in being with other people. It's a feeling that they're in some way 'like us'. Establishing a feeling of rapport is vital in business. We're much more likely to do business with people we feel comfortable with. Once you're in rapport you can get away with discussing potentially tricky subjects because everyone involved will feel more aligned with each other. Sometimes rapport happens within seconds, but on other occasions we have to make it happen.

case study Yuko says: "When I hold a business meeting, the first thing I do is to make sure I am in rapport with the other people there. I always try to sit at a 90° angle rather than directly opposite. If you sit in this position it is then very easy to copy the curve of their spine and also to take note of where they are breathing from; their lower abdomen, mid-range or high up in their chest. I start with whoever I think is the

■ **Matching and mirroring.** When two people are in rapport they subconsciously match each other's body language, from posture and vocabulary to vocal qualities and key words. That's why, when we are in rapport, the other person feels so similar to us. Whereas mimicry feels like mockery because it is within our conscious awareness, matching and mirroring is subtle and largely subconscious.

Watch other people who are getting on well and you will see how it works. One person folds their arms, the other person follows. One person leans forward on the table, the other people around do too. Matching means you follow the other person identically. Mirroring means that you are the mirror image of the other person.

Here's what to match to create rapport:

■ Key words, tone and speed of voice, facial expressions, posture, gestures, head tilt, even breathing speed.
■ The quickest match is posture. Match the angle of the sitting or standing position, and watch the results.

Get rapport in your daily work life by matching and mirroring other people's voice qualities and body language.

leader in the group. If I get rapport with them then others automatically follow us without realizing. I will suddenly see a group of us sitting in the same way, maybe all folding our legs or leaning in the same direction. I know I'm in rapport also because I get a feeling of comfort with everyone at the meeting. If someone in the group accidentally breaks rapport, I know immediately because the feeling changes."

3.2

Pay attention

If you want to know what effect you are having on others, pay attention to them. That includes paying attention to tiny changes in other people's body language as well as what they are actually saying.

You need to pay attention to many things for successful communication. Some people regard communication as a one-way process and think that if they say something then the other person will fully understand and accept it. However, sometimes people don't understand, or disagree with, the other person, but don't dare say so. Or they feel that their own viewpoint is dismissed or misunderstood.

As well as paying attention to what the other person actually says, look out for small, but important *changes* in their body language, even if you don't understand what they mean. These are some of the tiny shifts in other people's body language that are most easily observed:

■ **Breathing and skin tone.** Watch their breathing rate and location (i.e. lower abdomen, mid-range or high up in their chest), skin colour (it may change from light to dark or shiny to non-shiny or vice versa).
■ **Lips.** Observe the lower lip size – tiny shifts make the lips appear thinner or more swollen.

one minute wonder When you start talking to someone, check body language for rapport or perhaps signs that might suggest they don't really mean what they say. Notice what kind of words the other person primarily uses – are they visual, auditory or kinesthetic (see Secret 1.4)? Be flexible with your own words, voice tone and body language.

■ **Eyes and face.** Pay attention to the other person's eye focus and pupil dilation as well as the symmetry or asymmetry of their facial muscles. (Secret 3.3 explains more about subconscious eye language.)
■ **Voice.** Listen to variations in the qualities of the voice. Notice the voice tone, tempo and timbre, pitch and speed.

The object of these sort of observations is not to start interpreting them immediately. Facial expressions are not universal and it is dangerous to generalize too much. For example, if someone is frowning are they irritated or concentrating? You won't know until you get to know the person well, but what you can do is notice shifts and changes and see if you can observe any patterns. For example, if you notice a change every time you mention a particular subject, you can then ask something like, "Do you need more detail?" or "Are you comfortable with this?"

A useful attitude to adopt is that *you* are responsible for the impact of communication. If you don't take responsibility, your impact on others is going to be mixed. If you do take responsibility, you're likely to increase your impact and have improved business relationships.

Pay attention to both verbal and non-verbal signs to check that your message is getting across.

3.3

Watch the eyes

People can't disguise their eye movements, and if you can learn how to read them you can tell a lot about what is going on inside their heads.

This is very useful in business when talking to colleagues or selling to clients. As well as knowing which sense you prefer to use, by watching people's eyes you can work out other people's preferred sense. This allows you to talk to them in their language.

You can observe what senses are being used by asking questions and watching people's eye movements as they think about the answer. Practise on your friends:

1 When their eyes move up and to their right they are making a visual image in their mind. Ask them, "What would I look like with a hat on?"

2 When their eyes move up and to their left they are remembering a picture of something. Ask, "What does your bedroom look like?"

3 When their eyes move directly to their right they are imagining what something would sound like. Ask, "What would a mouse sound like singing happy birthday?"

"The eyes are the windows to the soul" Anonymous

4 When their eyes move directly to their left they are remembering a sound. Ask, "What does your mother's voice sound like?"

5 When their eyes move down and to their right they are feeling something. Ask, "What does cashmere feel like when you touch it?"

6 When their eyes move down and to their left they are talking to themselves. Ask them to tell themselves a joke.

In a business context – for example if you are selling to a group of people face to face – watch the eyes when you describe your product. Not everyone will respond in the same way. Check out who is relating to you when you use different words and expressions. Feed the imagination by using a mix of visual, auditory and feeling words (Secret 1.4).

■ If they are mainly using the visual sense to process what you are telling them, then make sure you use lots of visual description and show them the information they need.
■ If they are using the auditory sense, then describe in detail the benefits of your business.
■ If they are using feeling, then use kinesthetic words – perhaps give them a brochure to hold.

People's eye movements can reveal if they favour the visual, auditory or kinesthetic sense.

3.4

Don't mention the blue tree

When you read the title of this Secret what do you think of? A picture immediately formed in your mind of a blue tree, didn't it? So don't think of a blue tree. Stop thinking of a blue tree right now! What happens when you really try *not* to think of a blue tree? You still have the picture.

Your brain works with images and recreated memories. Feed it an instruction and it will make a mental picture of what you have told it. If you say, "I wonder what such and such smells like?", your brain obligingly hunts around until it finds a stored memory of something as near as possible to that smell. If I ask you, "what does Happy Birthday sound like?" your brain will hunt around amongst your memories to recreate that stored sound.

The brain loves pictures especially. When I tell you to think of a blue tree, it can imagine what a blue tree looks like because it has a picture of a tree and of the colour blue. Hey presto... all it needs to do is to put the two together.

It's the same if I ask you to do something. For example, "Come with me to the park." Your brain makes a picture of us going to the park and thinks, "Do I want to do this?" If the answer is "yes", then you feel happy and motivated.

But hang on a moment. Didn't I just ask you *not* to think of a blue tree? True, but the brain doesn't like negatives – it can't make a negative picture. It still makes the picture of the tree first. If you really don't want me to think about something then it's best to tell me what you *do* want me to think about instead. "Do think of the yellow tree."

You can imagine how important this is when you communicate in business. If you want your boss or client to feel positive about your ideas or about you, use positive descriptions and imagery. They are making pictures of what you say all the time so make sure you leave them with the images you intended.

Choose your language carefully and make sure you use positive words to create positive images.

3.5

Create a positive state

Everything that goes on inside you – your internal feelings and thoughts – has an effect on your communication. What you think and believe about yourself and the world, as well as about people you meet, will 'leak' into your body language.

Excellent communicators all have one thing in common: they are all able to maintain a positive state. To put it another way, when they want to communicate positively with their words, they make sure that the message that their body language and voice gives is aligned – or what NLP calls 'congruent'.

Have you ever met someone who was saying all the right things, but just didn't feel right? Perhaps they were selling or presenting to you or training you. Their message should have been positive because the

one minute wonder If you can't remember a specific episode of feeling confident, authoritative etc, then just imagine what it would be like if you could feel like that. Step into this visualization. Make sure you are experiencing it as if it were happening to you right now and you were seeing the scenario through your own eyes.

words were positive but their body was saying something else – perhaps showing a lack of confidence, or depression, uncertainty or annoyance.

To communicate positively you need to bring your emotional state under control, because negative emotions will leak into your body language. If you've got a positive message, you need to be in a positive emotional state when you deliver it. Because the mind and body influence each other, there's a very quick way to create this.

1 Think of the state that would be most useful to you. What do you want to feel? Confident? Alert? Curious? Authoritative? Energized?

2 Now remember a specific time in the past when you felt what you want to feel now.

3 Immerse yourself in the memory. This means experiencing it as if it were happening to you right now. Imagine yourself there.

4 As you experience the memory, really see what you saw, hear what you heard, feel what you felt. You will find that your emotional state changes.

5 As soon as you get the feeling of the other emotional state, your body language will change. You may walk taller, change your facial expression or sit straighter.

You can do this in a matter of seconds any time you are not feeling what you want to feel.

Re-enact a memory of a positive emotional state to feel it again now in both your mind and body.

Be a great motivator

The world's best business people are motivators. They need to be great readers of people's subconscious wants and needs. There is something about the way they talk to you that just strikes a chord, hits the right buttons and gets you going. Think about who you'd like to motivate. Is it yourself and also others? Could you become a great manager, coach, salesperson or employee? You can use these NLP secrets in any of these roles.

4.1

Discover your direction

What motivates you at work? Are you more driven by what you want to achieve or by what you want to avoid? How about the people around you? It isn't necessarily a clean choice between one or the other. Sometimes people are a mix of both.

There is a set of subconscious motivators we have that influence our day-to-day behaviour. These are known in NLP as 'meta-programmes'. How we motivate ourselves – by moving towards something or away from something – is an important meta-programme. The easiest way to discover your own motivational direction is to ask a simple question: "What do you want out of work?" What is the first answer which comes into your head? Is it something you want to have, do or be, or something you *don't* want?

case study Ken says: "I sell properties overseas. When talking to potential buyers, I use different tactics depending on what seems to motivate them. Some people like to picture a possible exciting future in the property. Their imagination gets going when I show them lots of pictures of a property in the brochure and on the website. I encourage them to talk about how

■ **'Towards' people.** People who are motivated by moving towards a reward talk about what they want rather than what they don't want. The way to motivate them is to show them the rewards or results they will get by going along with your view. If they know they can get more of what they want through you they are going to be happy.

■ **'Away from' people.** People who are motivated by moving away from things they want to avoid tend to give this away in their language e.g. "I just want to avoid getting poorer, mucking up again, taking on more stress." To influence them, tell them how your idea, product or goal will help them avoid what they want to avoid. For example, "If we do this as a team it's going to reduce the amount of time we all need to spend working each day."

If you are not sure, or you think your colleagues are a mix of 'towards' and 'away from' people, make sure you cover both options every time you sell an idea. Tell your team what you want to avoid and achieve with what benefits. "Here are our objectives. This is what we want to be careful to avoid, and just as importantly these are our goals."

Find out if you're generally motivated to move away from what you don't want, or towards what you do want.

they might see themselves there. Other customers are more motivated by thinking about the disappointed feelings they will have if they don't buy the property. Some people make up their minds based on what they think other people will or won't say if they do or don't buy the property. It's amazing how motivational talking the right language is."

4.2

Know the reason why

Are you full of 'shoulds', 'oughts', 'need tos' and 'have tos'? Or do you talk more about future 'possibilities', 'opportunities', 'chances' and 'choices'. Listen to yourself and your colleagues over the course of a day and notice who uses which words. You'll notice that patterns begin to emerge.

In the average office, a lot of grumbling tends to go on. Many people don't feel they have choices in life or at work. Instead they think that life is about having to do things. Somehow choice is for others or doesn't even exist at all.

There are two types of people you will encounter. Those who do things because they feel they have to and those who do things because doing them opens up other possibilities.

The easiest question you can ask to find out which motivates another person is, "Why are you choosing to do what you are doing in your business life?" You can add, "Is it because it gives you choices and possibilities or because of a sense of obligation and that you have to?"

The person will either reply with a reason or series of reasons that are about what they can do or what they feel they have to do. In other words, their answers to this question will be mainly about necessities, possibilities or a mixture of both.

one minute wonder Listen to the words and phrases people use when talking about what's important to them on any subject. Use their language when you tell them about the benefits of your idea or product and you'll find them motivated to help you or buy from you.

In order to influence either type, talk to them using the words they use. For example, imagine you want to persuade a colleague to write a major report with you.

■ **Motivated by necessities.** To a colleague who seems motivated by necessity you could say, "Think about what we have to do for this client. We really must do this to fulfil our obligations."

■ **Motivated by possibilities.** To a colleague who seems to be more motivated by possibilities you could say, "Imagine all the new opportunities that are going to open up once we do this report. There are so many possibilities."

■ **Motivated by both necessities and possibilities.** Try a mixture of both tactics to present a really strong case to a colleague who seems driven in both motivational directions: "Think about the possibilities here and also what we have to do to fulfil our obligations."

Listen to different people in your office. Who talks of possibilities and who is driven by necessities?

4.3

Be convincing

If you look inside a newspaper you will sometimes notice that a company runs several versions of an advert in the same edition. This is because the more times you see the advert, the more convinced you're likely to be about its message.

Everyone's convinced by different means, or what's known as their 'subconscious convincer filter'.

When other people do things in a way that fits with your convincer filter, you'll be confident that what they say is true. They're then going to be able to motivate you easily. When you buy into an idea or buy something from a sales person, you may think it's all been about logic, but really it's happened because they've matched your convincer.

one minute wonder Wait a while before calling when you've got a client who takes time before they're convinced. Then phone and say, "It seems a long time since I spoke to you, almost as if it's... [the time they take to be convinced]". Then talk about your product or idea – they will buy it.

"The key to successful leadership today is influence, not authority"

Ken Blanchard

Imagine you are selling the idea of a new product. Here's an easy way to find out what the other person's convincer is. Ask them:

- What would it take to convince you that this is a good idea?
- Would you need to see how it went over a certain period of time? If so, how long? Weeks, months? How many?
- Would you need to see more material about it? Hear more about it? Try it out yourself? How many times?

Most people are either convinced by getting the information a certain number of times (often three) or over a period of time. Use words that draw on their imagination to motivate them. "Can you imagine what it will be like after [e.g. six months] when you have experienced this idea? How convinced will you be feeling?"

Some people have an automatic convincer. You don't need to convince them, they buy straight away. For some it's how the information comes – by seeing, hearing, touch. If so, show them, tell them or let them experience your idea, as appropriate.

But occasionally a person doesn't fit into one of these categories and may be hard to convince. If you meet such a person, tell them, "I know you will not be convinced until you find this out for yourself". They will then respond positively.

Identify how many times or over what timescale you and others need to be persuaded before you're convinced.

4.4

Reward interests

Do you know who is interested in what type of activities in your team? Who prefers to work alone? Who prefers to work with data? Who of your team members likes action and who is more reflective? If you get people doing things that interest them, they will naturally be motivated to do more.

What are you mostly interested in? Activities, information, people, places or things? If you look at your life you will find that one of these has tended to motivate you more than others in the past. This is your 'primary interest'.

■ **Activity** If you are working on a project with someone who is interested in activity, tell them how it's going to work.
■ **Information** If you are interested in information, you need to be motivated by being told 'why' and 'what' the project is about.
■ **People** For some, who they will be working with is the first thing they want to know.
■ **Places** For others, the location is all important. Tell them where the project will take place.
■ **Things** People in the final group just want to know about things – what they'll be working with in the project.

"All successful people are big dreamers. They imagine what their future could be, ideal in every respect, and then they work every day toward their distant vision."

Brian Tracy, motivational coach

You may find you have a mix of people in your team so make sure when you sell to your colleagues that you talk about what's important to them, not just to you.

Now, do you know who likes to work independently, who likes to be in charge and who likes to be in a team? The best way to motivate each of these types is to feedback your understanding of their preference, whether or not you can indulge it. Say:
■ "I know you like to work independently and that's why I want you to…"
■ "I know you like to manage people, so…"
■ "I know you prefer to work with the team, therefore…"

Finally, be aware of who likes to get stuck into activity straight away and who needs time to reflect.
■ For those who are activity driven, you will motivate them by saying something like, "Let's get on with this idea straight away."
■ For the reflective, tell them, "I know it's important for you to have some time to look at this. Take the time you need to make the decision."

If you've a team member who needs time to reflect before taking action, give them space to stay motivated.

4.5

Offer the right sized chunks

In any given group of people who work together, there will inevitably be some who like lots of detail about a project, while others, if given too much detail, will tend to switch off and get bored? A 'chunk' means the amount of detail a person can handle hearing or dealing with at one time.

NLP divides people into two broad types: Specific and Global.

■ **Specific** There are those who prefer to be specific in the level of information they take in. They focus on the details.

---

case study Shirley says: "I was training a group of IT professionals and I was very enthusiastic about the new technology. But about halfway through I started to notice that the group was getting bored. I couldn't understand why because I had given them lots of variety in the training and we were discussing interesting theories about it. After the .break one of the

---

■ **Global** These people like the big picture. They move rapidly away from detail towards more abstract or global chunks of information.

If you want to motivate specific thinkers to do a project with you, give them details. Sometimes they need a bit of the big picture, but you soon gauge from their impatience that they want to leap into detail. The key words for you to use for these people are: "Here are the details."

However, that's just what's really going to switch more 'global' thinkers off your project. So what you need to say to them is "Here's the big picture." If you are not sure then ask:

■ How much detail do you need at this point?
■ Would you like me to start with the big picture and move on to detail?
■ Shall we keep this at an abstract level?
■ Shall we keep this at a detailed level?
■ Would you prefer me to start with detail and move on to the big picture?

Remember that this is an entirely subconscious motivation. You can't make someone with a big picture filter become a detailed filter or vice versa, but you can use what's on offer to motivate them effectively.

Give an appropriate level of detail when you talk to your team or clients.

group started to ask detailed practical questions. It was at this point it dawned on me. Whereas I love theory because I am an academic and I develop this stuff, these guys just wanted detail, detail, detail so they could work out how they were going to use it. I left the theory and started talking about application and the energy levels in the room rose immediately.

4.6

Separate externals from internals

Think about how you know when you have done a good job. Do you feel it inside and feel satisfied enough with that, or do you need someone else to say something positive before you can feel satisfied?

Can you answer these questions?

■ How much are you influenced by what other people think?
■ What motivates you? Do you have an internal frame of reference, an external reference, or a bit of both?

If you are having difficulty answering the above questions, think back to the last occasion when you know you succeeded at work. What was it specifically that let you know you had done well? Did you just have an inner knowing that you had succeeded, or did you wait until you got positive compliments or feedback from your boss or your co-workers before feeling confident that you had done well? What about other occasions?

one minute wonder Find out how enjoyable managing other people is for you. How easy is it for you to know how to make yourself more successful? What about other people? Would you know how to tell them how to increase their success rate? Are you only able to help yourself or do you have the ability to help others?

■ **Internal people.** Some of us are totally internal in our frames of reference. If you have colleagues or clients like this, the only way to convince them of anything is to feed this fact back to them to show you understand what type of person they are. You could say to them: "Only you know for certain whether this is right for you…you'll know inside what you think."

■ **Externally influenced people.** If on the other hand the person is externally influenced you can say something like:"Think what other people here will think about this / you doing this."

■ **People who are motivated by a mix.** If you want to cover both bases, since some people are motivated by a mixture of both, say: "Think about what you think and what others think…"

Work out if you and your colleagues use internal or external frames of reference.

4.7

Manage mismatchers

Have you ever met someone who found fault with everything you said? They contradicted, picked an argument or disagreed on every level. Yet other people seemed to be happy with what you said. The first person is a mismatcher.

When you are in rapport with other people they match you by agreeing with you easily. When someone is mismatching you on the other hand, they are out of tune in every way.

■ **Motivating matchers.** Some people love matching without thinking about it. These people instinctively see similarities in life. When they start a job they think: "Oh this is like other jobs I have had before". In a work situation these 'matchers' don't tend to like changing

case study Serge says: "I was managing a new team of business analysts. There was one who had been there for a long time and I had been warned that he could be difficult. Actually he was very friendly but every time we had a meeting he'd pick holes in the other analysts' thinking. Sometimes he was right, but the problem was that he would do it at the beginning

work frequently so it's easy to recognize them. You'll find them contentedly working away at the same work year after year. To motivate a 'matcher' all you have to tell them is: "As you think about this you'll see that this is the same as you're already doing / having."

■ **Motivating mismatchers.** Mismatchers are good at spotting what's different. They notice what doesn't add up about what you say or what you do. As a result they look to disagree. In order to motivate them, you need to buy into their way of seeing things by saying something like: "You probably won't believe this" or "I don't know if you will believe this." By using a negative phrasing they will naturally want to disagree with what you have just said. Their first instinct will be to think: "Well, actually I do believe this." By allowing them to disagree, you'll find them wanting to match you after all.

■ **Dealing with slight mismatchers.** If they're only a slight mismatcher, you can say: "You may find that this is mostly the same and a bit different from what you've done before – which will probably make you want to do this." To find out who's who in your team, ask: "When you start a new job what do you notice first? Similarities or differences?" The answers will be enlightening.

Give mismatchers roles where noticing difference is useful in your business.

of the meeting, which demotivated everyone, and the meetings dragged on. What I gradually realized was that he was trying to be helpful and couldn't help noticing discrepancies. Therefore, I gave him a new role as sub-editor and told him to use his contrary voice at the end of a meeting to make sure we hadn't missed any major future problems. This suits everyone."

4.8

Respect values

If you demonstrate that you value someone else's values, they are going to be very happy with you. If you are their manager, they'll want to keep on working for you. If you are selling to them, they'll want to keep on buying from you. If you're their employee, they'll want to keep you on their team.

Values are a valuable thing. If you find out what someone's values are treat them with great respect, as you would a precious piece of jewellery. If you trample on someone's values they are going to be as unhappy as if you had broken their most valued possession.

To motivate someone to buy from you, show them that you understand and will satisfy their values. There are four stages to this.

one minute wonder To ensure motivation, businesses need to align their values with their employees' values. To motivate a team, all the team members' values need to be aligned. Find out the values of the business and each team member. What can you do to make sure all your values are met?

"We confide in our strength, without boasting of it; we respect that of others, without fearing it"

Thomas Jefferson, US President (1801–09)

1 First, find out what is important to them according to the situation – their business generally, or what they consider important about a product or idea. You may get 'towards' and 'away froms' (see Secret 4.1).

2 Since they will probably name more than one value – people, success or quality, for example – ask them to rank their values in order of importance. "Which is more important to you? X or Y?"

3 Making sure you use their value words back to them, ask them to define those values. "What exactly do you mean by 'quality'/ 'people'?"

4 Ask, "How do you know when you have X, Y or Z? What does that mean to you? What is your evidence procedure for…? Why is this important to you?"

Always use the same key value words the other person uses.

Dig deeply and find out why different values are important to motivate at a deep level.

Boost your performance

There are likely to be many times when you and your team face personal blocks to performance. Luckily, there are many solutions and techniques that you can use to help yourself and others through difficult situations. The advantage of all the performance-boosting secrets in this chapter is that they are simple and quick to learn yet yield extraordinarily effective and lasting results.

5.1

Believe in yourself and other people

The beliefs you have about people, your abilities and business in general will determine the results you get in business. If you believe that you can do something you will find a way to do it. If you believe that people like you can't be successful, then you probably won't be. Change your beliefs, and change your success.

Here's a useful belief that many effective people hold to be true:

■ People work perfectly (and that includes you).

When perfect people do something wrong it's not because there is something *wrong with them personally* but because their *behaviour is not useful*. The same goes for you, if you don't perform how you would like to. Thinking about people and performance in this way stops us demonizing others or beating ourselves up. It means that you can separate what *people have done or not done* from *who they are*.

"Believe and act as if it were impossible to fail"

Charles F. Kettering, American inventor

Think of it the opposite way round. People who don't have this belief see a colleague do something in a particular way and think something like, *that's so typical of that person* or *that means they are…* . This way of thinking is counter-productive to building good relationships. If you are a manager and think about your employees in this way, what's going to happen? Would you want someone to think about you like this?

It's more useful to think that you or your colleague is always doing the best they can and simply may need to change the way they do things to get different results.

■ The effective way to create change in behaviour is to change the way you think: you will create different results.

Imagine that your subconscious is just waiting for new information and new instructions. Imagine that it has been running certain programs like a computer for years and years. Load up new software and you're going to get different output. The programs you were running were effective, but they were out of date and not as user-friendly as the new ones.

■ Now choose some useful new beliefs.

What you believe may well come true, so believe something useful.

5.2

Change your perspective

Let's face it – people don't always get on. Where a conversation hasn't gone as planned or there is a block to resolution, see what happens when you 'try on' the other person's perspective. This technique is very simple but powerful.

Think about two people: you and a person who has a different opinion than you about a subject. Practise this technique first of all in a situation where there has been a small disagreement or difference in perspective rather than a big one. With practie, you'll find this easier and easier and you'll get used to seeing events from three perspectives: yours, the other person's and the viewpoint of someone who is totally detached from the situation.

one minute wonder Hold a mirror in front of you. What does the you in the mirror see when they look back at you? How are you presenting yourself in business? Think not so much about your appearance as about what attitudes come across from the person in the mirror.

"If there is any one secret of success, it lies in the ability to get the other person's point of view and see things from that person's angle as well as from your own" **Henry Ford, American industrialist**

1 Imagine you are sitting in a chair looking at them sitting in another chair. Ask yourself: "What do I see, hear, feel and think in this position about the interaction?"

2 Then imagine sitting in their position looking at you from their point of view. Ask yourself: "What do I see, hear, feel and think in this position about the interaction?"

3 Now, imagine you are standing at a distance between the two of you, being an observer. What do you notice as a detached observer about the relationship and interaction between you and the other person?

Each position will bring fresh insights. Do a round of the three positions first, then go back to each position again to see if this brings any additional perspectives. As you gain insights, think about what you want to take on board and use as a resource in the future.

If you use this exercise frequently you will find that it really helps you overcome blocks with colleagues and opens up your thinking. These benefits will directly feed through to your business performance and success.

Practise looking at life from other perspectives to avoid conflicts.

5.3

Change your negative thoughts

Do you encourage and motivate yourself like a good leadership coach? Or do you push and punish and beat yourself up? What happens when you face a challenge at work? Are you negative or positive?

A negative person sets off on a goal and then thinks, "I'm not good enough to do this" or "this is bound to fail" or "my clients don't like me". Here's a powerful tool for changing these sabotaging thoughts.

■ In your mind, see your negative thought as an image.
■ Is the image light or dark, framed or unframed, small or large, moving or still, in colour or in black and white? Are you in or out of the picture?

---

case study Eleanor says, "I had a voice in my head every time I had to stand up and talk at my company meetings. I used to get really nervous. I realized that my 'self talk' was really cruel. I said things to myself such as, "You're no good at this and everyone's laughing at you." It really was talk too – a voice in my head that sounded a bit like an old teacher I had.

> "For those who believe, no proof is necessary. For those who don't believe, no proof is possible."

Stuart Chase, Economist

■ Now see what happens when you change the picture. Make the image smaller and darker, move it away from you, if it is framed make it unframed or vice versa. Experiment.

You will find that you feel differently about the thought when you change the way it is stored in your subconscious. We call these different aspects of the image 'submodalities'. Making a negative image smaller, darker and further away works for many people in reducing the strength of the thought.

Do the opposite with a positive thought. Create a mental image for "I always get what I want. I can do it." Now make the image larger and brighter, move it towards you in your mind, if it is framed make it unframed or vice versa. Experiment. Change the colours. Make it warm and friendly. See what works.

Notice how you feel now.

Minimize negative mental images.

I changed it by first turning down the volume. Then I changed the voice so it sounded a bit silly, like a cartoon character talking. I sped it right up until I couldn't take it seriously at all and I made it friendlier. The voice had sounded as if it was from the left side of my head so I changed it to coming out of my big toe. Now I just laugh whenever it tries to talk to me!"

5.4

Change the frame

A central belief of NLP is that all meaning is 'context-dependent'. This is just a way of saying your view might change if you see things in a different light or if your perspective is reframed.

Here's an example. You wake up late one morning and miss the train to work. What does this mean? Well it rather depends who's looking at the situation. If you have an important meeting you might think, "This is terrible. My business is ruined today." But what if missing the train meant that you missed an accident? You would think "How lucky. I am a fortunate person."

■ **Change the frame.** This idea is like changing the frame on a picture. When you look at a picture through a small frame, big frame or different coloured frame, you will see it differently. The frame you put

one minute wonder "I'm too..." or "he's too...", "I wish I could do this more..." are complaints that someone is a particular way in a particular context. Change your perspective by thinking where the behaviour would be useful. E.g., "He's too sensitive to be a manager." In what job would sensitivity be useful?

> **"If I have the belief that I can do it, I shall surely acquire the capacity to do it even if I may not have it at the beginning"** Mahatma Gandhi, Indian leader

on things changes their meaning because it changes what aspect you pay attention to. Nothing has meaning in and of itself. We give it meaning.

Think about a tricky situation you are in or have experienced recently. How would other people react to the same experience? What positives might they gain from the experience that you've overlooked?

■ **The situation is not absolutely negative.** You have given it a negative meaning. If you choose to see it differently you can choose to give it a positive meaning. Negative emotions about an event are not caused by the event itself but by your response to it. By changing the frame, you can create positive emotions and new choices.

For example, suppose you miss out on winning a client. It seems a disaster in the short term but in the long term you are able to win a bigger competitor as a client who is only willing to do business because there is no conflict of interest.

How do you change your view? Change the situation, time-frame or context. Ask: would the meaning be different?

Meaning depends on context, so if you don't like the meaning of something, 'reframe' it.

5.5

Anchor positive feelings

You see a red traffic light and automatically stop. You smell something that brings back a childhood memory. The tone of someone's voice triggers an emotion. These are examples of subconscious anchors.

Anchoring is a way of linking a strong feeling to a visual, sound, touch, smell or taste stimulus. Anchors can last for years. Although many are created naturally, you can also create anchors intentionally to bring positive feelings in whenever you need them. They are used very successfully to achieve goals in areas such as sports and business.

1 First think of a situation where you would like to feel positive. Name the feeling which would be most useful, e.g. powerful, happy, excited.

case study "There are several ways I use anchors in a training situation," says Michelle. "First, how I dress acts as an anchor. If I wear my best suit I feel more professional. Then I have a 'lucky necklace'. I know there's nothing special about it, but I've anchored good feelings to it. In the training I use objects, pictures and music that I know trigger good feelings in most people.

2 Think of a specific time in the past when you felt this feeling. Absorb yourself into the memory so that you experience it again.

3 As you feel the feelings strongly rising up to a peak, clench your fist, press your thumb and finger together or touch your knuckle. This is your anchor. Hold it for a couple of seconds and release.

4 Repeat steps 1–3 three to five times. You can revisit the same positive experience or another one with equally strong, positive feelings. Intensify the feelings each time.

5 Break concentration and think about something else for a moment.

6 Now 'fire your anchor' with your fist or by touching your knuckle or wherever else you set the anchor.

7 By triggering the physical anchor, you will automatically experience the feelings you have linked to it. How do you feel about the situation now?

Anchors are a way of creating a good feeling whenever you need to feel positive or energized.

If I want people to feel relaxed I play soft classical music. I also use violin music for more meditative sessions. Then if I think energies are flagging I put on upbeat, fast music. It immediately changes people's state and gives them more positivity. But one thing I never have in the room is tissues, because people subliminally associate tissues with feeling miserable!"

5.6

Change your language

How you describe a situation to yourself inside your head influences what you feel about the situation. Words are very powerful. Think carefully before you speak. What message are you sending yourself about you and your own success?

Negative self talk has a big impact on how you feel about yourself. Imagine you have just given a good sales pitch.

■ **Not feeling confident.** You might say to yourself, "I was lucky, but it won't be repeated. This is not me. It was just a fluke. Well that's the last time that will happen."

■ **Feeling confident.** You might say instead, "I can do this again now and get better and better. This is the new me."

"If you realized how powerful your thoughts are, you would never think a negative thought"

Peace Pilgrim, American peace activist

one minute wonder Here's a quick way to distract yourself from negative thinking. As soon as you become aware of a negative thought, break the pattern. Interrupt the automatic thought by clapping your hands, humming to yourself or pinching your thigh. You will distract yourself and break the thought pattern.

Or imagine you had just talked to your boss and he said you hadn't performed as well as expected on a task.

■ **Not feeling confident.** "I always muck up. I can't improve no matter what I do. Typical me."

■ **Feeling confident.** "This was a one-off. I'll do better next time. It was not typical and I'll succeed next time."

If you choose to talk to yourself using negative and critical language you just boost unhelpful beliefs about yourself. Repetition tends to reinforce beliefs, so if you say things enough times they become habit forming. Negative beliefs feed into negative behaviour and attract unhappy experiences. Before long, you end up with a bank of negative memories forming, which provide the justification for thinking of these beliefs as 'fact'.

By changing your self talk, you can reverse the process, setting up new, positive experiences to anchor positive feelings for the future.

Change the language you use to and about yourself and you will see that it feeds through immediately to boosting your performance.

Use positive language to talk to yourself and reinforce your success.

5.7

Respond positively to criticism

Being able to stand outside an experience can be useful if you tend to get overly emotional in work situations. Emotions can stand in the way of us achieving our goals. Many successful people have the ability to detach or dissociate themselves from difficult situations, including criticism.

Dissociation is a way of distancing yourself from negative emotions. Over two-thirds of people respond to criticism by having immediate negative feelings. The emotions are usually so uncomfortable that any useful feedback is lost. If you would like to hear feedback comfortably, use dissociation. Next time you are feeling something you don't want to feel follow this method:

 Imagine stepping outside your body as if you are viewing your body from the outside, as in a film. You can even put some transparent glass up between you and the other person in your mind.

 As soon as you do this, feel yourself becoming detached, calmer and more relaxed.

one minute wonder The opposite of detachment is association. To associate, just bring the feeling into your body and experience it as if it is fully happening to you NOW. Use this to imagine new behavior in future in which you incorporate any useful information from the feedback you received.

 As the person speaks to you, stay as an observer. Imagine the words printed out at arm's length from you or at a distance from you in some other way. Perhaps bouncing off the glass?

 As you remain detached, make a picture / film of the feedback in your mind. Now compare that picture in your mind with a picture of any other view you have of the situation.

5 You can evaluate the feedback versus the alternative view and see if any parts of it make sense. If it does, say, "Thank you for bringing this to my attention."

6 If the feedback is vague, gather more information. Useful feedback is specific.

 Use the information in the criticism to decide how you will behave differently in future, if appropriate.

You now have the choice to stay objective about any situation. Simply dissociate or detach from the feeling and you will be much more powerful in business as you learn from the feedback or criticism you are likely to receive from time to time.

Mentally standing back from criticism is a way to use it as useful feedback.

5.8

Be your own success coach

Many successful businesspeople have boosted their performance and stretched themselves to achieving their goals by coaching themselves to success. Anyone can improve their performance by making small but continuous improvements each day, each week, each month and each year.

Excellence in any discipline can be broken down into a series of small steps over a period of time. Current research suggests that it takes about 10,000 hours of practice to be a leader in a field. That may seem a lot at first, but break it down over your career life and you'll see that it's not so much to achieve mastery of your area.

one minute wonder Create a mental picture of your outcome that has sound and feeling attached to it. If you've already experienced in your mind what your goal will feel like when you achieve it, you'll really go after it. If it's just a couple of lines on a piece of paper, you won't.

"Develop success from failures. Discouragement and failure are two of the surest stepping stones to success." **Dale Carnegie, self-help guru**

Remember when you first learnt something? Perhaps to drive or ride a bike? It seemed hard to begin with but after a while it became so easy and subconscious that now you don't even think about this as a skill. Use this simple structure to determine where to focus your energy:

■ Do I have long-term and short-term outcomes for my career and business?

■ What am I focusing on today, this week, this month?

■ What is the one thing I can do now that will make the biggest difference to achieving this outcome?

■ What have I learnt today or what can I learn today that will make the biggest positive difference to me achieving this outcome?

■ What will I do with what I have learnt today, this week, this month? Where and how will I use what I have learnt in a positive way?

■ What new actions can I take? Which will make the biggest positive difference to me achieving this outcome?

■ How will I measure my progress towards achieving my outcome?

You can coach yourself to success over days, weeks and years.

5.9

Model excellence

When you were a child did you ever wonder what it would be like to be someone else who you admired? Did you imagine what they might be thinking? How they might be seeing the world differently? If we want to achieve what others achieve we need to think like them.

NLP came about when Richard Bandler and John Grinder learnt how to 'model' or think like successful therapists, working out the key factors that allowed them to get great results.

You can apply this same principle to business. If you don't know how to do something, you can learn how to do it by modelling someone else who does it already.

one minute wonder This is a useful technique you can use to model yourself – to find out how you do some things successfully so that you can get similar results in other areas. Think about something you do well. Question yourself to find out what you think about this area. How is this different to your thoughts about other areas of your work or life?

"Responsibilities gravitate to the person who can shoulder them; power flows to the man who knows how" **Elbert Hubbard, American writer**

It is important to choose someone who is excellent at what they do. There is no point in aiming at mediocrity.

■ First think of the person you want to learn from. This doesn't have to be someone you know directly. You can choose a prominent public figure who you have seen on TV or read about.

■ In your mind, step into their body and ask the question: "If I were you what would I be thinking and believing about myself and the world. What would have to happen for me to think like you?" (If you know the person you can of course ask them directly.)

■ Examine their behaviour, beliefs, values and other motivators as well as their preferred representational system.

■ Some of these thoughts may be relevant and some irrelevant. You want to discover the key thinking processes of the person that make the difference between being OK and excellent.

■ Think for each, "If I didn't have this, would I get the same results?" If the answer is 'yes' then you don't need it. If it is 'no' then you do.

■ Once you have found out the vital elements you can learn the same beliefs and other ways of thinking and learn the same ways of behaving.

Borrow attitudes and beliefs from achievers in your business.

Make a powerful impression

According to surveys, the majority of people are afraid of standing up in front of a group and presenting. They get tongue-tied or nervous and don't present the information they have as well as they could. But if you want to lead, then you need to be able to speak in front of your peers, clients and managers. Use the secrets in this chapter and you can unleash the impressive presenter inside.

6.1

Learn from the masters

You may know someone personally who is a good presenter: perhaps a friend or colleague. Or there may be someone in your general business area or in public life who you admire. What is it this person does that makes them a great presenter?

Whoever you think of, they probably have a few things in common with other excellent presenters. By learning some basic techniques that all presenters use either consciously or subconsciously, you too can learn to make a great impression, whether that's in front of a small group of colleagues in a meeting or at a conference in front of thousands, or in any other situation.

one minute wonder A great presenter is always alert to feedback and open to new knowledge. A useful belief to adopt is, "I can always learn something from everybody I meet in business." This belief keeps the brain flexible and supple and means that the presenter can learn and incorporate new ideas into his or her behaviour.

1 First of all be clear about what you want to say and why you want to say it. In other words, use outcome-based thinking.

2 Make sure you know the audience's reason for being here and focus on what's in it for them.

3 Accept responsibility for getting your message across. The onus is on you to make sure the audience has understood.

4 Control your state of mind so that you have positive thoughts and emotions when you stand up and talk.

5 Be aware of your own verbal and non-verbal communication (body language) at all times, as well as your audience's.

6 Make sure your non-verbal communication actually matches your verbal communication.

7 Be a flexible communicator. Pay attention to the language (visual, auditory, kinesthetic), values, beliefs and other motivators of your audience.

8 Match and mirror to keep in rapport. Be aware and notice if there are any 'mismatchers' in your audience.

9 Stay curious about people, passionate about your subject and enthusiastic to teach others about what you know.

Focus on your audience's reasons for being at the meeting and satisfy their 'what's in it for me' desires.

6.2

Use stories

A young boy wanted to be the fastest skier in the world. He lived on a desert island, so he set out one day on a home-made boat. After weeks he reached a vast land with snow-covered mountains. As he rested on the beach he met an old man who told him the secret of how to reach his dream…

Our subconscious loves stories. When we hear a story we listen at a deep level. A good story gives us a warm feeling inside and brings out ideas. For example, with the short story above, you may begin to wonder what was the secret. Your brain starts to make possible pictures.

Stories increase your impact when you present. Instead of giving endless PowerPoints with information, use stories to illustrate points or ideas. Your audience can identify with the characters in the story and they then open their minds to take in the message you want to give them. Stories overcome resistance because they talk to the right side of the brain: the part of the brain that is sometimes known as the artistic brain. This part of the brain loves images and symbols. By telling stories we bypass logic – the left side of the brain – and engage the imagination instead.

one minute wonder Choose a story about a subject your audience relates to and a central character the listener identifies with. Relate each feature of the idea you are selling to a feature in the story. Use rich images to stir the imagination. Keep the language positive and use a mix of visual, auditory and kinesthetic words to appeal to different people.

■ **Seek out examples.** If you look at all the great teachers, orators or philosophers, they have all used stories to engage their audience and also to get a message across as simply as possible. Think of well-known fairy stories from your childhood.

■ **A story can be very simple.** A common idea in business is fighting the competition or overcoming difficulties to triumph against the odds or perhaps winning a race. Think of a real story or make one up.

■ **Have a strong character and storyline.** The story you tell doesn't have to be directly about a business, but it does need to have a character your audience will be interested in. The path of the story mirrors the path you want your audience to think about and has an ending which fits the outcome you want them to take on board. The best stories get the listener to look in a different way at an idea or situation.

Use stories to stir the imagination and get your message across to your audience.

6.3

Vary your voice

How flexible are you in the way you talk to people?
Are you aware of how fast or slowly you talk? Do you
always talk in the same way or do you notice yourself
changing when you talk to different people? Can you
sound both empathetic and assertive, for example?

When you talk to someone, over a third of your impact comes
from your voice. As you give information and tell stories your audience
will be listening to how you say what you say as well as what you say.

Be aware of when you want to sound authoritative and when
you want to reach out to your audience, perhaps to ask a question.

■ **A question.** The questioning tone means that your voice rises at the
end of the phrase or sentence.
■ **A statement.** The tone is flat throughout the phrase or sentence.
■ **A command.** Your voice goes down towards the end of the phrase
or sentence.

Which do you use most often? Each provokes different reactions
in your audience. If you are giving facts, it's good to use a statement
tone. If you want to open up a response from the audience you might

one minute wonder Use your breath to help you have flexible communication. Visual people tend to speak fast as they breathe from high in the chest. Auditory people are slightly slower, breathing from the middle of the chest. Kinesthetics are the slowest, taking deep breaths from the stomach. Practise all three and see what happens to your voice.

want to use a questioning tone. If you want to shut down discussion, you may want to use a command tone. Listen to other people when they talk. Which do they use and what reaction does it get?

Now think about the other elements of your voice:

■ Pace, tone, speed, volume, and other general qualities (for example how gravelly or how smooth your voice is).

Remember, if you want to enjoy rapport with your audience, you need to be able to match them with your voice as well as with your body language.

What do you do if you have a large group audience? Well, make sure that, as well as talking using words from the different representational systems (Secret 1.4), you also vary the speed of your voice. When you first start talking get the audience's attention by speaking fast and with energy. Slow down a bit and then more to capture the whole audience, then vary your voice throughout your speech.

Practise varying your voice so that you can be flexible in your communication.

6.4

Use the 4-Mat system

A good speaker is focused on the audience and has a structure planned for reacting to different parts of the audience. One way to do this is to use what is known as the 4-Mat system, developed by educational theorist Bernice McCarthy.

This system lets you talk to different types of people in a group based on their different learning styles. The theory is that when people listen to a talk they divide into four types who ask four different types of question: 'why', 'what', 'how' and 'what if'? If they don't get the answers they want to their main question then they switch off.

■ **'What' learners.** They want to know facts, concepts and details.
■ **'Why' learners.** They like to know why they are there and why they need to listen to you.

> **one minute wonder** As well as using the 4-Mat system for talks, it is extremely useful if you ever do business training. Structure your training for all the groups. You will end up with a good balance of information, reasons why, demos and practical exercises, as well as plenty of time for questions.

■ **'How' learners.** They want to do something and put what you are telling them into practice.

■ **'What if' learners.** They want to try out different ways of doing things and think about other options as well as the consequences of doing it one way.

If you want your whole audience to engage with you, then there is an ideal order in which to structure your talk and make sure you engage with all four groups.

1 First explain why the subject you are talking about is important. What is the reason for the audience to listen and learn? You can ask the question: "So would this be useful to you?" Keep explaining 'why' until you get a definite 'yes'.

2 Then go into the facts and information for the 'what learners'. Ask as you go, "What else do you need to know at this point?" Go into as much detail as needed to satisfy your audience.

3 Now satisfy the 'hows'. Show how your information can be used. If you are training you can give an exercise to do. Let your audience engage with what they are learning if possible. Ask: "What else do you need to know to use this?"

4 Engage your 'what if' learners by letting them explore options and variations by having a question and answer session.

Structure what you say to take account of the four different learning styles.

6.5

Run a great meeting

Often in business we need to take part in company meetings or meet with clients. It will help you to control your impact in either situation if you have a clear structure for meetings, such as this one.

 1 First of all decide why you want a meeting. Is it necessary? What is the desired outcome and how will you know when you have achieved it? Could you achieve it with a phone call instead?

 2 Have an agenda that focuses on your outcome and evidence for achieving it. This will keep everyone on track in the meeting.

 3 Choose a meeting place that has positive associations or anchors and preferably is used only for meetings so the people taking part subconsciously get into the right mindset.

 4 Start the meeting by stating your outcome for the meeting and evidence for achieving it. This starts everyone off from the same place. Make sure you've got everyone to agree to this.

 **5** Keep the discussion relevant. If it goes off track, ask how what has been said relates to the outcome agreed. Because they have bought into the outcome at the beginning it is easy to stop side talk.

one minute wonder Obey the two-thirds rule. This applies in two ways. First of all, anyone coming to the meeting needs to be able to make a decision or contribute to two out of three agenda items. Secondly, if two-thirds of relevant people aren't at the meeting then cancel it.

6 Give people roles to play. For example, if you have someone who tends to pick fault and disagree, ask them up-front to be the person who plays Devil's Advocate at a pre-planned point.

7 Summarize as you go. As you agree on points, make sure you get nods round the table. "So we're all agreed on this point?"

8 If you need to clarify a point then backtrack by saying, "I would like to ask you to return to this point so we can come to an agreement on it."

9 If there is disagreement on a point use your negotiating skills. Here's an easy way to get agreement. Say, "If I do X then will you do Y?"

10 At the end of the meeting, summarize what you have agreed on and also agree on a next step.

Summarize points as you go and be an effective meeting leader.

Sell to anyone

Much of business is about selling something – either a product or a service to a client, or selling your skills and ideas. Why do you 'buy' one presenter, manager, product or service over another? It's because the person satisfies your needs – not just through the information they give you about their product or service but the way in which they do this. The NLP sales secrets here contain many elements that can be adapted for any business situation.

7.1

Know your client

When you first meet a business client you have an idea of what you want to persuade them to do or buy. They may be starting from a very different place from you. Your needs and outcomes may be different. If so, you need to find a win-win solution so you both feel good about the sale.

Knowledge is your most powerful sales tool. Most salespeople know their product but not their client. In selling you need to think like your client and know their needs. Why someone buys is not always why they think they buy. They might say it's because of quality, service or technical reasons but actually it's because subconsciously they think: "If I own X product I will have Y need fulfilled."

The real need to buy is subconscious. It could be for something to look, feel, taste, smell or sound a certain way. Or by owning this product, it's to see ourselves being, doing or having something. Your job is to find out what the need is, then to get your buyer to use their imagination so they can see themselves satisfying the need they have.

"Business opportunities are like buses, there's always another one coming" Richard Branson, British entrepreneur

Here's the basic structure for all successful selling.

1 First, establish rapport so the client trusts you. Then question and gather information about why the client needs your product or service.

2 The question you need to be able to answer is: "For what purpose does he / she want it?"

3 If there is no need, you must walk away from the deal because you can't get a win-win situation.

4 However, if there is a need, your job is to link the benefits of your product to the client's need.

5 Make sure you have asked the client to agree that your product matches the need. You can then ask the client to buy.

Follow this simple structure and you'll be amazed how much more successful you become as a salesperson, either when selling to clients or when persuading colleagues to go along with your ideas.

Identify the benefits of what you are selling and what your client needs in order to make a match.

7.2

Ask questions

Questioning is one of the most powerful selling tools that you have at your disposal. You need to gather information about your client's beliefs about you, your business and your product, their needs and hidden motivations for buying, as well as any possible objections they might harbour.

Here are some of the types of questions to ask:

■ **Outcome.** "What specifically do you want as an outcome?" (Could be a thing or a feeling.)
■ **Reason why.** "What does this outcome mean to you?"
■ **Evidence.** "When you have it what will it be like? What does it look, sound, feel like? What is your ideal X? What features does it have?"
■ **Timing.** "When and where do you want it?"
■ **Motivation.** "What really motivates you to buy something? How do you usually know that it is time to decide to buy?"
■ **Convincer.** "When was the last time that you were really convinced by a purchase that you made?"

All these questions provide useful information. For example, if your client says to you, "That car is not good value", he is saying that

one minute wonder Suppose you have asked all your questions but for some reason there is a block. Here is a very useful line of questioning you can ask yourself and / or the client. Ask, "Why don't you have it already?" "Is there anything that is stopping you having it now?" The answers will help you to find out hidden needs, benefits and motivations.

his need is to have good value. You can ask him to give you more information: "How would you know if it was good value?" or "How would you know if it was not good value?"

If your client has a problem coming up with why they might want to buy your product, then you can get them to delve deeper again through questioning.

■ **"Do you know anyone who has one already?"** Find out what the client feels that does for the other person.

■ **"Have you ever had something similar that you really liked?"** This reminds the client of a positive past experience and assists them into a positive state for buying.

■ **"What did you see/hear/feel when you had it?"** What benefits did it give the client.

By asking questions in this manner, you focus on your client's model of the world – what is important to them. Once you have established their underlying beliefs and motivations you can then start to show how your product or service matches what they are looking for.

Asking questions stops you making false assumptions about what your client needs and wants.

7.3

Check out what's important

Remember that values are our hidden motivations. Everyone's values are different and they are enormously powerful. If you can show how what you're selling will help your buyer to get more of their values fulfilled then they'll be eager to buy as quickly as possible.

■ **Identify the client's values.** It's simple to discover what's important to your client when buying. Just ask questions like: "What's important to you…

    ■ … about owning this type of product?"
    ■ … when you choose to make a purchase?
    ■ … when you take on a new supplier?"
    ■ … generally when you do business with someone?"

There are lots of different variations of the same question. The key is to get your client to feed you all their 'values' – those vital motivational words. Once you use those words back to them and relate them to what you are selling, you will be making them very happy. In fact, each time you show them how they're going to get more of what's important to them, you can imagine what is really happening is that you are lighting up the part of their brains that gives them a positive feeling, a bit like turning on the lights on a Christmas tree.

■ **Show how your product or service fulfils those values.** So your client says: "You know, what's really important to me here is the quality of the product, and the aftercare…" Explain how your business prides itself in building longstanding relationships and spending a lot of money on research and development to ensure that you get the quality of the product right in the first place, but also so that the after-care is there. (We'll assume that your business does indeed pride itself on these things.) If the client is not convinced, then dig deeper again. Find out what quality or after-care means to the client. You can then respond: "Let me explain exactly how we can satisfy those criteria and why they are just as important to us."

If you're still not getting anywhere, it's worth asking, "Is there anything more or equally important to you that we haven't covered?" This question will reach any deeply subconscious values the client may have.

Find out your client's values because once you can fulfil them you will make a happy sale.

7.4

Paint a happy future

What would your life be like when you have what you really want? The things you want to own? The place you want to live? The person or people you want to be with? What will that future look like and feel like? And how do these type of questions light up your imagination?

■ **"What will it be like when...?"** This is a highly powerful question to ask someone because it catapults them into an imaginary future. Imagine you're with your client. You've found out what their needs and values are. You've told them a bit about how your product can help meet these needs and fulfil what else is important to them. Now you want to get them to take those warm fuzzy feelings about the product forwards in their minds so they start to see themselves as if they have

one minute wonder There are some other words you can use to stimulate pictures in someone's imagination: "Consider what it would be like if..." "What would it be like if..." "Imagine a scenario..." "Paint a picture of..." When people hear these words, they immediately respond by imagining a new future.

> "Successful people are always looking for opportunities to help others" **Brian Tracy, business guru**

already 'bought' from you. This will help you to seal the deal. "What will it be like when…

- … you own this?"
- … you have done this?"
- … you have this in your possession?"
- … you have achieved this?"

"Will you feel a certain way? Look a certain way? Be able to be or do or have something?" By asking these questions, your client immediately starts to see pictures of themselves, either with the product or having done what you are urging them to do. This happens so immediately that they can't stop it happening even if they wanted to. The imagination is too powerful for that. The power of your questions will help them to form clearer and clearer pictures.

■ **Picturing the decision to buy.** You can also use the imagination to get your client to think about how they will make the decision to buy. Let's assume you have already bought X, how did you know it was the right product to buy? What told you it was a good decision? This allows the client to play at owning the product in their imagination. It also overcomes any resistance they may have about not wanting to make an instant decision about buying from you.

Use the "what will it be like when?" question to help fire your client's imagination.

7.5

Get agreement along the way

When you talk to a potential buyer, it's no point carrying out a conversation and then waiting until the end to ask them to buy. It's much more effective to get their agreement all the way along, so they can't turn around at the end, after you've used all that effort, and say "no".

■ **Collect yesses.** Great salespeople collect yesses. As soon as you start to discover what your client is looking for, tell them how features of your product fit their needs. Then, ask them to agree with you. "Can you see how that feature would be of value to you?" You are looking for a "yes". Make sure you get agreement on every criterion.

one minute wonder There is a great technique called the Conditional Close, which is an easy way to close a sale. Ask for agreement once certain conditions are met. For example, "So we've agreed on the colour and the price. If we get a larger size shall we deliver it on Wednesday?"

"People who produce good results feel good about themselves" Ken Blanchard, leadership expert

■ **Add tag questions.** "Can you see how the aftercare we give would meet your specifications?" Listen for a "yes" or a nod, then build on this. Adding a 'tag question', like "isn't it" or "hasn't it" or "don't they" at the end of a sentence usually makes the other person nod or say "yes". Half the time it's subconscious. This happens quite often, doesn't it? See what I mean? Yes? Did you catch yourself nodding or wanting to agree just then?

Once your client has nodded a few times, they're on your side. However, do be careful. You need to have built up lots of rapport before using tag questions, and use them as reinforcers rather than as a first step to agreement. If you use tag questions too early – before you have matched some benefits of your product to the identified needs – then you might get a "no". So choose your timing before saying: "It is good value, *isn't it?*" "This does save time and money, *doesn't it?*"

■ **Ask at least three times.** A lot of people are convinced by hearing things three times, so make sure you collect at least three yesses or three nods before you start thinking that the buyer is probably on your side.

Don't wait until the end to make the sale; make the sale all the way through your conversation.

7.6

Talk your client's language

What happens when the sale has been going pretty well, but the client starts to raise an objection or to delay? One vital thing to check is that you are using the right language for that client.

■ Use sense-related language. Essentially, if a client raises an objection, they haven't got a positive feeling yet about what's on offer. If you talk the same language as your client you'll hit the mark, be in tune with them and help them to see the benefits more quickly. See what I mean? Did I grab you just then? Did you like the sound of that? As you probably noticed, I used a mix of visual, auditory and kinesthetic language in those last points. Which language is your client using?

---

case study Here is how John, a car salesman, uses three languages when selling. "Hear me out about this car. You may find what I say to you rings a bell straight away and it sounds like something you would really like to buy..." (auditory); "I would like to show you some images of the car so that you can clearly see all the

---

■ **Appeal to visual people.** Suppose your client says: "I still do not see any good points in your product." They literally don't see any, because their mental picture does not contain any. Clients using lots of visual words will pay close attention to how you look when you're presenting. Take care with your appearance and also the appearance of the room you are presenting in. Show pictures and drawings, charts and graphs: anything that is a visual draw for your product.

■ **Appeal to kinesthetic people.** The client says, "I'm not sure what I feel about your product." You reply: "Notice how it feels." Let them touch or hold the product.

■ **Appeal to auditory people.** The client says, "I'm not sure about the sound of your product." You need to make your product 'strike a chord' by using auditory words and phrases. The tone of your voice will influence the decision.

Use visual, auditory or kinesthetic language to appeal to your client.

benefits and get a picture of what it will be like after you buy it. As you can see, it comes in a range of bright colours..." (visual); "I feel that this car is one you are going to want to grab hold of straight away. Touch the smooth texture of the metalwork. Feel the comfort of the leather interiors..." (kinesthetic).

7.7

Handle objections simply

Most objections raised by potential clients fit into a few categories. Once you know how to handle these then you are well on your way to becoming a natural salesperson and master persuader. The secret is to keep your responses simple and structured.

There are a few simple steps you can take to handling barriers to making a sale.

1 Create rapport. Make sure you listen fully to what the other person is telling you. Repeat what they say using a questioning tone. "You really think it is too expensive?"

2 Find out whether this is the only reason that the person doesn't want to buy. If it is and you answer the question fully then the person will agree to buy.

3 Show the person fully what the value of the product is and create a sense of urgency to make them want to buy now.

These are two of the most common objections and a reminder of what to do about them:

■ **Common objection 1.** "It looks good but I need some time. Let me think about it for a few days." The client may come back and buy or may be using this as an excuse to walk away and never come back. They are afraid of suffering buyer's regret. To solve this objection you should check your language again (Secret 7.6). Does the client need to see more, hear more or perhaps actually handle the product? Have you satisfied the client's convincer strategy (Secret 4.3)? Have you dealt with their values and showed how your product can fulfil them (Secret 7.3)?

■ **Common objection 2.** "It costs too much. I just can't pay that sort of price." Here your potential customer is saying that this product isn't offering enough value (Secret 7.3). What you need to show is that it will cost the client more not to buy the product now, or to show how the product is a low cost in relation to what it will earn. For example, "If you have a phone that has an internet service you can keep in touch with colleagues while you are travelling. That will save you a fortune by making you productive while you're away."

Handle objections by answering your client's real questions.

7.8

Use power words

Some words are more powerful than others. Clever salespeople use these words scattered through their language as they are speaking to clients. All the customer knows is that they feel good. See what happens if you start using power words when you sell.

■ **The power of naming.** Salespeople are often taught that using someone's name is very powerful (along with nice manners and saying "please" and "thank you"). This is one of the first power words you have at your disposal.

However, here's a note of caution, as using someone's name can be overdone. The thing about power words is that they must never be intrusive. So, although I will reveal some very powerful words here, make sure that you are subtle in the way you use them. Bring them naturally into your conversation and don't over-emphasize the word each time you use it, otherwise it will simply sound irritating.

■ **'Because' is a great word to use.** When we hear the word 'because' we think we are about to hear a very logical reason. "The reason this is worth taking another look at is because…"

one minute wonder Use the word 'new' cautiously. Many people like to be at the forefront of what is new and exciting, and own more of it than the rest of the population. But the desire for new things varies between age groups and cultures, so make sure you add other values. For example, new technology needs also to be secure and, at times, good value.

■ **'Clearly, obviously'.** Again, doesn't it sound logical when someone starts a sentence in this way. "Clearly if you begin with the word, obviously it must be obvious, mustn't it?" These words work because they overcome resistance. Our minds relax and listen to what's coming next.

■ **Universal values words.** These have a positive effect on the majority of people too. Here are some of the most powerful values words you can use to advertise your business: proven, benefit, trust, fun, money-saving, investment, healthy, new and exciting, comfort and security, new discovery, happiness and joy, powerful results, value.

Although you have your own business values and indeed life values, there are some things which are pretty much important to all of us. We all want to feel positive when we buy something. Many of us want to eliminate risk and have some assurance of security. Look out for adverts and see how some words recur again and again.

Choose powerful words, but don't overuse them.

7.9

Watch your 'buts'!

On a final note about powerful words, bear in mind that the word 'but' is a very powerful negative word and should be avoided. Many of us litter our speech with 'buts' when we should be using 'and' instead, especially when we want to sell.

"On the surface your business looks as if it is very profitable, but I want to take a look at the figures." "Your business appears to be very profitable and I want to take a look at the figures." There's a lot of difference between the way we hear these two sentences, isn't there? The 'but' in the first sentence immediately rings a bell of alarm.

What a difference a small word makes, doesn't it?

one minute wonder In Secret 2.2, we discussed problems about the word 'trying'. Here we'll reiterate that if you add a 'try' to a 'but', you're in big trouble. "I will try to make the product cheaper for you, but..." You're not going to make a sale with a sentence like that in your verbal negotiations.

"There's a great power in words, if you don't hitch too many of them together"

Josh Billings, 19th-century American humourist

Here are some more examples:

■ "I would like to buy your product, but I want to handle it first."
■ "You did very well at making sure the project was successful, but I would like you to take another look at the output."
■ "Thank you for coming to the interview. You have many of the skills but…"

Each time you hear a 'but' you know that what's coming next is going to take away from what went before. When you hear an 'and' on the other hand, it adds to what's gone before. Here's another example:

■ You did very well at making sure the project was successful, and I would like you to take another look at the output.

Be careful with what you say when you're selling (or indeed in any other conversation). As soon as you catch yourself saying 'but', your client is going to hear it as a negative. If you use buts you may undo all the good sales work you've been doing.

Keep your language positive to make the outcome positive.

Jargon buster

Anchor
Stimulus or trigger associated with a specific response. For example, a smell is anchored to trigger a positive emotion. Can be visual, auditory, kinesthetic or associated with smell or taste (olfactory, gustatory).

'As if'
NLP 'frame'. Acting as if and therefore thinking as if some response were already in place. Changes emotional state.

Association
As though you are seeing a memory through your own eyes happening to you right now.

Auditory
Relating to the hearing sense.

Behaviour
The actions and reactions we take in the external world relating to people and the environment.

Behavioural flexibility
Having a broad range of responses to life and people rather than habitual responses so that you can achieve results you haven't achieved before.

Beliefs
The general statements we hold true about ourselves, the world, other people, meaning and identity, which guide our perception of reality.

Calibration
Learning to observe other people's non-verbal language and subconscious responses.

Congruence
When all a person's subconscious and conscious responses are in alignment towards an outcome.

Deletion
When a person subconsciously excludes portions of the world from their internal representation.

Dissociation
Looking at yourself in a memory / internal picture as if you can see your whole body – like watching yourself in a film.

Distortion
An internal picture that is different from what it represents.

Eye-accessing cues
Movements of the eyes representing types of thinking.

Generalization
A mental representation of an experience that the mind uses for a whole category of experiences.

Internal representation
Information we store internally in the form of pictures, sounds, feelings, smells and tastes.

Kinesthetic
Relating to the body and feelings.

Map of the world / reality
Every individual's unique mental representation of the external world.

Matching
Copying other people's behaviour / body language to produce rapport.

Mirroring
Matching behaviour in a mirror image.

Modelling
Observing, analysing and replicating the successful behaviour and thinking of others.

Outcomes
Desired states or goals.

NLP
Neuro Linguistic Programming – a series of techniques that help you modify your behaviour in order to achieve greater self-motivation, better communication and organizational skills.

Perceptual position
A particular viewpoint or perspective.

Presupposition
A useful assumption or belief to adopt.

Rapport
A feeling of trust and chemistry between two or more people.

Reframing
Changing the framework around the meaning or context of information to give it a different meaning.

Representational systems
The senses: seeing, hearing, feeling, smelling, tasting.

Sensory acuity
The ability to be highly observant and make fine distinctions in the information we process through the senses.

Strategy
The set of steps (internal and behavioural) that produce specific outcomes.

Submodalities
The specific building blocks and qualities of each of the senses, for example volume, tone and pitch for the auditory sense.

Timeline
The way we internally store our past, present and future images.

Visual
The sense of sight.

Visualization
Making an internal image or picture.

Well-formed conditions
A mental construction of an effective outcome.

Further reading

Alder, Harry *Handbook of NLP: A Manual for Professional Communicators* (Gower, 2002) ISBN 978-0566083891

Alder, Harry *NLP For Managers: How to achieve Excellence at Work* (Piatkus, 1996) ISBN 978-0749916435

Andreas, Steve, et al. *NLP: The New Technology of Achievement* (Nicholas Brealey, 1996) ISBN 978-1857881226

Bandler, Richard and Grinder, John *Frogs into Princes: The Introduction to Neuro-Linguistic Programming* (Real People Press, 1985, revised Eden Grove 1990) ISBN 978-1870845038

Bandler, Richard *Using Your Brain for a Change* (Real People Press, 1997) ISBN 978-0911226270

Beaver, Diana *NLP for Lazy Learning, How to Learn Faster and More Effectively* (Vega Books, 2002) ISBN 978-1843330493

Boyes, Carolyn *5 minute NLP* (Harper Collins, 2008) ISBN 978-0007266593

Boyes, Carolyn *Business Secrets: Communication* (Harper Collins, 2010) ISBN 978-0007324446

Boyes, Carolyn *Need to Know? NLP* (Harper Collins, 2006) ISBN 978-0007216550

Dilts, Hallborn, and Smith *Beliefs: Pathways to Health and Wellbeing* (Metamorphous Press, 1990) ISBN 978-1555520298

Knight, Sue *NLP at Work: The Difference That Makes a Difference in Business* (Nicholas Brealey, 2002) ISBN 978-1857883022

McDermott, Ian, and Jago, Wendy *The NLP Coach: A Comprehensive Guide to Personal Well-being and Professional Success* (Piatkus, 2002) ISBN 978-0749922771

Molden, David *Managing with the Power of NLP: Neurolinguistic Programming, a Model for Better Management* (Financial Times / Prentice Hall, 2000) ISBN 978-0273707912

Molden, David *NLP Business Masterclass* (Prentice Hall, 2001, 2nd ed, 2007) ISBN 978-0273707905

O'Connor, Joseph *Leading with NLP, Essential Leadership Skills for Influencing and Managing People* (Harper Collins, 1998) ISBN 978-0722537671

O'Connor, Joseph, and Seymour, John
*Introducing NLP: Neuro-Linguistic
Programming* (Thorsons, 1999, rev. 2003)
ISBN 978-1855383449

O'Connor, Joseph, and McDermott, Ian
Thorsons Way of NLP (Thorsons 1996)
ISBN 978-0007110209

Robbins, Anthony *Unlimited Power:
The New Science of Personal Achievement*
(Simon and Schuster, 1997)
ISBN 978-0743409391

Shapiro, Mo *Understanding Neuro-linguistic
Programming in a Week* (Hodder and
Stoughton, 1998) ISBN 978-0340711231

www.BusinessSecrets.net